Dedicated to the tireless army of people on their knees, who change the world quietly

Introduction...or how to use this book

Lent is a time to draw close to God in a variety of ways. This book is a series of reflections designed to engage the body, soul and spirit through a series of exercises. Each day has an opportunity to pause and reflect which can be read or explored more deeply.

To extract the most from each reflection, carry out the suggested activity with a partner or small group, so that your wisdom can be expressed, and you can learn from the wisdom of others.

Give yourself time - ten minutes is enough. God can speak to us in ten minutes and then walk with us all day.

Write on the book if you wish. Engage with it however you wish. The reflection space is for you to make notes, to draw pictures, to scribble or to leave blank.

Add to it. Miss bits that seem unimportant to you this year. Don't feel guilty about missing a day out. You can always do it next year!

If you have any further thoughts, email us at ian@blobtree.com or pip@blobtree.com

Ian and Pip

Day 1: give the picture time to speak to you.

Allow your eye to settle upon the Blob who feels like you do as you start your journey towards Easter.

Which Blob would you most like to be along this journey, and why?

What will you need to change to make this happen?

Prayer: draw a heart upon the palm of your hand in pen and ask God to help to guide you to become an agent of Love this Lent.

Reflections

Day 2: reflect upon the picture.

Allow God to show you which Blob is like you when faced with the temptation to run away from silence.

Which Blob is the next step you need to take towards hearing God for yourself?

Prayer: find a silent place, such as a car on your own, and spend five minutes in silence slowly drawing a heart upon the palm of your hand.

In the silence think about a relationship problem that is on your mind and hand it over to God to alter in some way.

Reflection

Day 3: colour in the picture

Allow your mind to consider the feelings of each Blob.

Colour in a Blob who struggles with the temptation to eat too much. Find a Blob who is how you feel about food.

Prayer: imagine that Blob climb into the palm of your hand and slowly offer it up into the healing presence of God's love.

Our emotions are linked to eating, but God is greater than our feelings.

Reflections

you

are a beautiful human person

Day 4: read these words

'You are a beautiful human person'

How does that make you feel?

Imagine God speaking those words over you.

Does that change how you feel?

Challenge: tell someone today that they are a beautiful human person. It's always true, even if their behaviour masks it.

Prayer: ask God to show you how much He loves you today.

Reflections

Day 5: look at the picture.

Imagine you were in a desert. Which Blob would you feel like?

Which Blob do you think Jesus felt like when He spent forty days in the desert? Why do you think that?

Action: sit somewhere different today and experience how it feels to be out of your comfort zone.

Allow yourself to go through the awkwardness. See it as a skill which you are developing - of not being afraid to be alone in a crowd.

Prayer: as you sit in a different place, pray for those around you to experience God's love.

Reflections

Day 6: read these words

'E m o t i o n   i s   o f t e n   c a u s e d   b y   m o t i o n'

When Jesus walked into the desert He took with Him all of His feelings.

They weren't denied or disallowed. When we walk with God our feelings are a part of our journey.

Are you aware of how your feelings change through an average day?

Action: keep a record of the different feelings you experience today - take note of what causes a change in your mood today.

Prayer: ask God to help us to read our feelings as signals, not to be controlled by them.

Reflections

Day 7: touch the picture as you look at it.

Which Blob is most like God in your opinion? Why? Which Blob is least like God in your opinion? Why?

Can you imagine God as all these Blobs or are there some you would definitely exclude?

Prayer: draw a heart shape over your chest and consider how others label us too simply...and how we can label God too simply too.

Action: write down the feeling words you have for God. Which are derived from the Bible and which relate to your current experience of life?

Reflections

Day 8: look at these words

'Our feelings are signals'

Think of the last time you got angry on the inside or out loud. What caused you to lose control?

Do you blame others for your feelings or do you try to recognise them and understand them?

Action: when you next feel angry choose to count to twenty before speaking...and see how that changes what happens. As you count, consider why you were triggered to become angry, not just what the other person did.

Prayer: touch part of your body that gets involved in angry outbursts or frustrations. Ask God to help you to understand the process in yourself.

Reflections

Day 9: touch your open palm.

We can either be a palm person - open and warm to others, or a fist - clenched and unyielding.

When Jesus walked into the desert he opened himself to God, and became willingly vulnerable.

Action: today, make an opportunity to touch someone on the back of the shoulder with an open palm and a word of appreciation, especially someone you do not usually touch in this way.

Prayer: ask God to help you to see when He touches your shoulder with His open palm of love today.

Reflections

Day 10: drink a glass of water.

Allow yourself the time to feel it moving through your body.

Water is refreshing in a desert place, it sustains us, allows us to live, and washes us clean.

Action: as you use water today thank God for its life-giving qualities. Each and every time...be surprised by the number of times we need it.

Each time you feel water on your body today, imagine God's work upon your life.

Prayer: ask God to wash us clean through the cleansing work of His Spirit.

Reflections

Day 11: run your fingers over your hands slowly

As we go into each day we have an opportunity to make each moment count.

Our touches can affirm the lonely, our pointing fingers can wound the emotionally vulnerable.

Action: during today take the opportunity to bless others who are usually isolated in our family, friendship groups and workplaces.

Be prepared for a negative response, as it is unusual for them to be valued by others.

Prayer: ask God to help you to befriend the lonely today...and beyond.

Reflections

Day 12: look into the picture

Touch the Blob which is how you feel when you are lonely.

Look at the other Blobs too. Some of them are your friends, classmates and family. We are often surrounded by people in their own emotional deserts. They have not been led there by the Spirit, but through being rejected by family and friends.

Action: watch the patterns of your family today. Do some of them spend almost all their time alone?

Is there a way you can spend time with them?

Prayer: ask God to help you to see the movements of others through their emotional daily experiences, not just their activities.

Reflections

Day 13: touch the Blob you are in an emotional fight

Have you ever had to give up the intimacy with someone you dearly loved?

As Jesus walked into the desert he knew that he was leaving the comfort of family life behind. He was facing a time of change. His mother, His father and His siblings were all left behind. His childhood friends became memories, nothing more.

Is there a Blob in the picture that is how Jesus was as He left home to begin His ministry, in your opinion?

Question: is there someone who you need to let go of in your life?

Is there someone who you are emotionally tied to who impedes your growth?

Or do you impede theirs?

Prayer: ask God to give you the strength to release that beautiful human person into the fullness of their life.

Reflection

Day 14: touch the object which causes the Blobs the most pain

When were you last in pain? What caused it?

When were you last in pain because of a right choice you made?

Jesus made a decision not to eat or drink, to purge himself. It was the right choice for that point of His life. It caused Him so much pain that the angels had to look after Him when He completed His mission.

Action: can you go without food for a day? Try to deny your body anything but water for twenty four hours. Note down how it affects you, and the thought journey which you take.

Don't feel guilty about not doing it if that is what you choose.

Prayer: ask God to speak to you today as you take control of your body by disciplining its intake of food.

Reflections

I'M MY OWN WORST ENEMY

LOVE YOUR ENEMIES

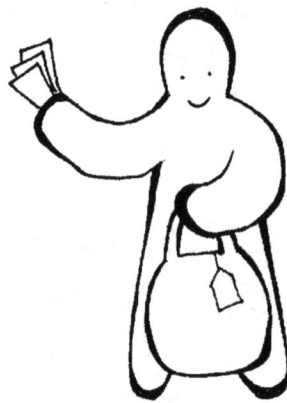

Day 15: reflect on these words:

'I'm my own worst enemy...love your enemies.'

Jesus never hated himself.

He showed self control and self respect.

When you make a mistake, how do you accept this is what people do, or do you put yourself down?

The time in the desert was a time to draw near to God, *not a time of punishment.*

Action: when we go through the day, take note of anytime you speak negatively about yourself. In your mind begin to repeat the healing words,

'I am a beautiful human person'.

Prayer: if God loves us, who are you to hate yourself? Ask God to release that same love within you.

Reflections

Day 16: touch your nose, your skull, your mouth and your heart

Getting to know ourselves is the journey of a lifetime. In the desert, without anyone else around, it is often easier to see who we are really like. For some of us we only see what is right before our nose. For others we think deeply about ourselves. As we get deeper, we listen to ourselves.

Finally we become aware of our feelings and can fully express these to ourselves and others. These levels of self understanding can be pictured from one to five.

One: our face – the outside, the superficial

Two: our mind – full of facts

Three: our mouth – where we express our opinions

Four: our heart – the centre of us – our feelings

Five: all of us – our feelings laid bare

Action : today, reflect upon which part of yourself you use most - your face, your mind, your mouth or your feelings?

Prayer: ask God to help you to become a whole human - using all of your being for His glory.

Day 17: touch the picture as you look at it

These Blobs are all in level 1 experiences, the basic human interchanges.

 Which ones do you do each day?

Could you deepen them with those individuals?

Action: find someone you usually say 'Morning' to and consider how to ask a deeper question of them. For example – 'What food do you enjoy? What's your favourite film/ TV series?' Moving deeper will take you closer to them.

Prayer: ask God to help you find a way to deepen a basic relationship.

Reflections

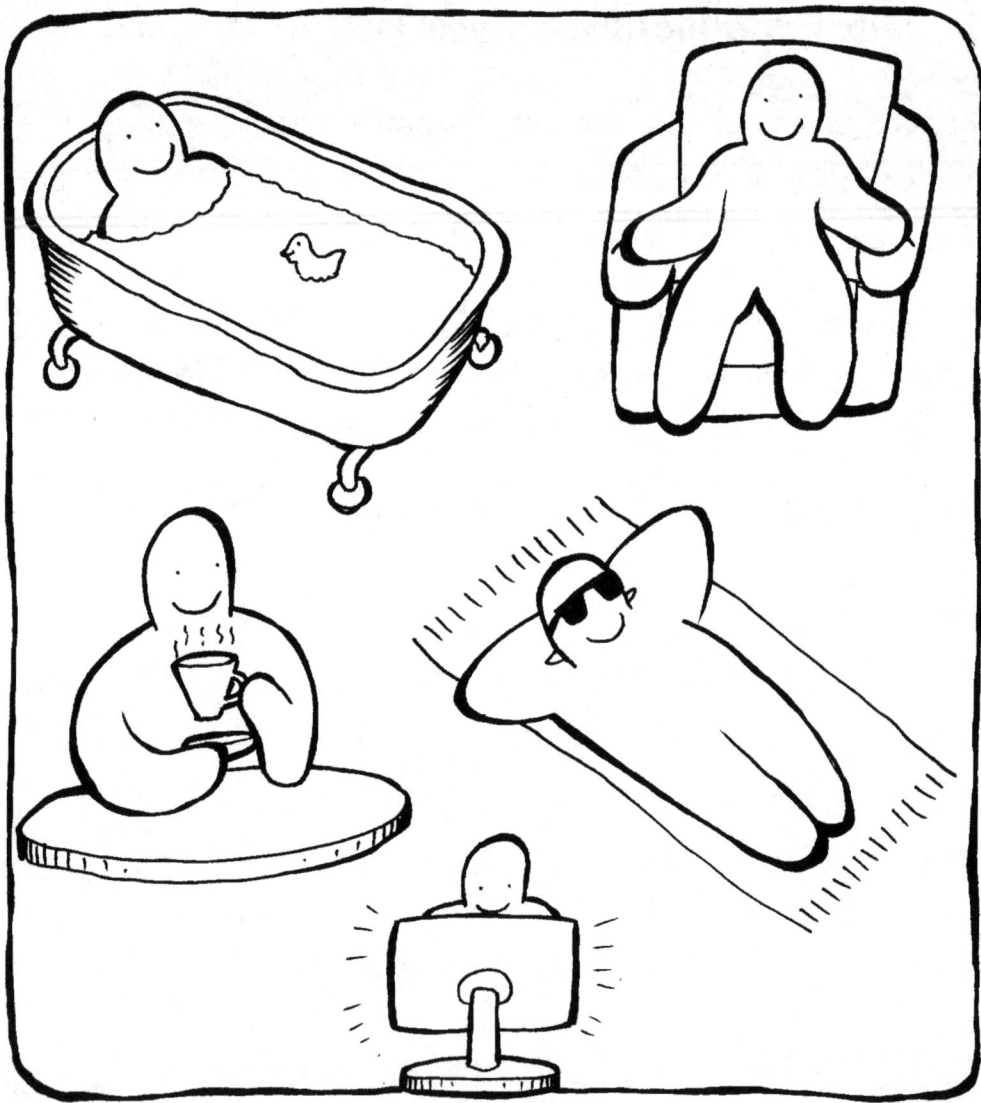

Day 18: run your hand through your hair

Something as simple an action as that can soothe us in the day.

We all have little ways that we comfort ourselves. In the desert there is no other comfort but Gods and our own.

Action: during today make time to be quiet and create a mini desert for yourself - perhaps relax in a bath, sit in your car, lie in your bedroom or close your office door.

In the silence repeat these words, 'I am a beautiful human person'.

Prayer: ask God to become your Comforter, the One whose words matter most to you.

Reflections

Day 19: reflect upon these words

'I am beautiful imperfection'

Yesterday we contemplated our beauty, today our imperfection.

The desert is harsh and clear. It reveals us as we are.

Can you cope with your weaknesses, and not run away from them?

Your imperfections are part of you, like visible scars.

You can try to deny them, but they won't go away.

See yourself as God sees you, with all your imperfections. He sees you, the unseen you, and still loves you. Can you do the same?

Prayer: ask God to show you how much you mean to Him, with all your imperfections.

Reflections

Day 20 look at the Blobs in this picture

Which ones would you feel afraid of?

Why would they scare you? Have you ever scared others?

Do you ever get scared by thinking about the supernatural?

When Jesus was alone in the desert He had the devil trying to tempt Him. The supernatural was very real to Jesus.

Do you ever consider what might be happening to you might have a supernatural background to it too? Or is that something you don't wish to consider?

Prayer: ask God to open your eyes to the unseen world at a pace which you can accept.

Reflections

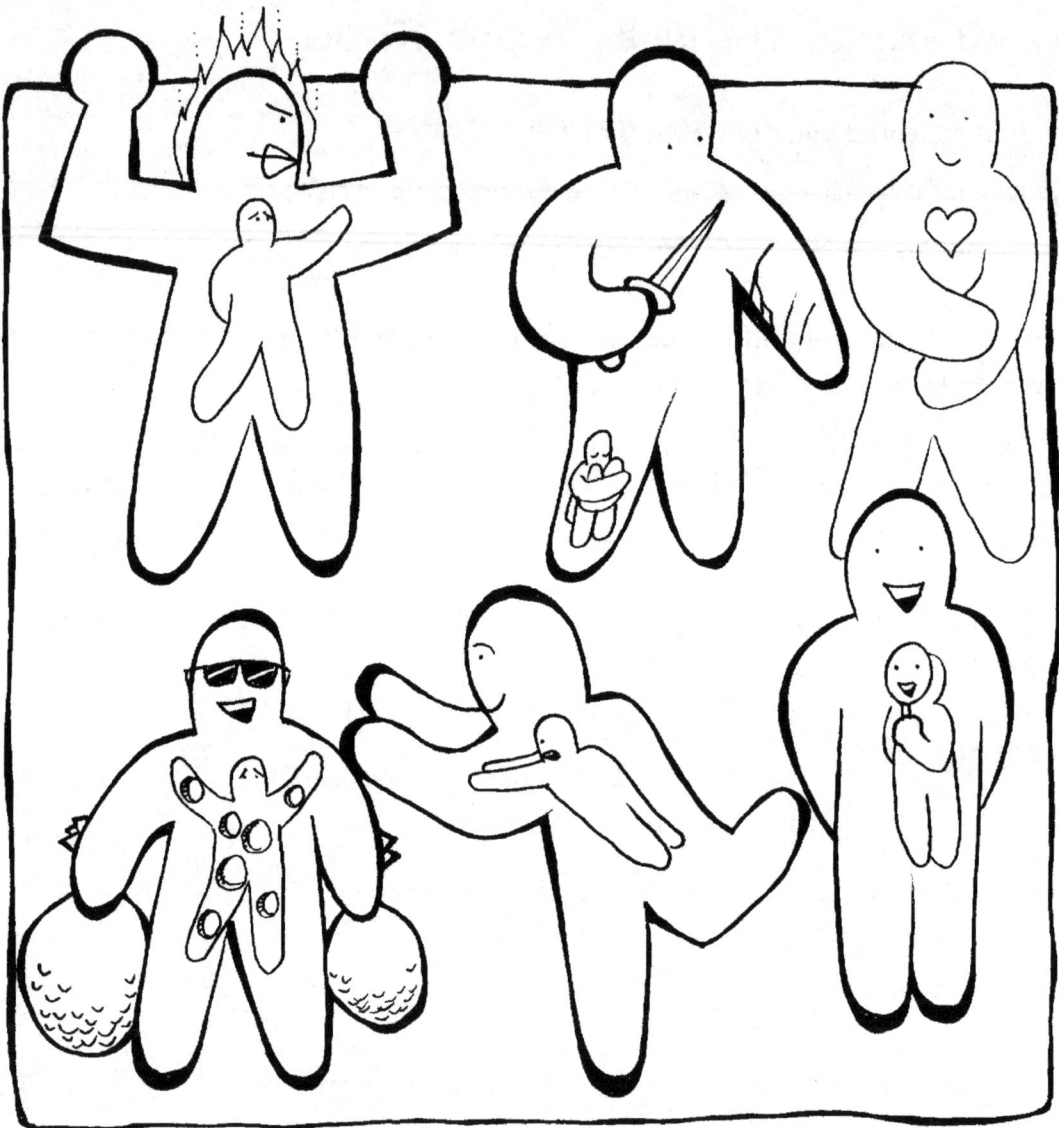

Day 21: reflect upon these words

'There is no difficult person, only difficult behaviour'

How do you feel about such a statement?

Have you ever felt angry because of the behaviour of others? Does that colour the way you relate to them? Have you ever made friends with someone who has difficult behaviour? How does it make you feel having such a friend?

Have you ever felt angry with your own behaviour? Do you ever wonder if people feel the same way about you?

Prayer: Dear God, help me to love others with the same love that You have for me whenever I let you down.

Reflections

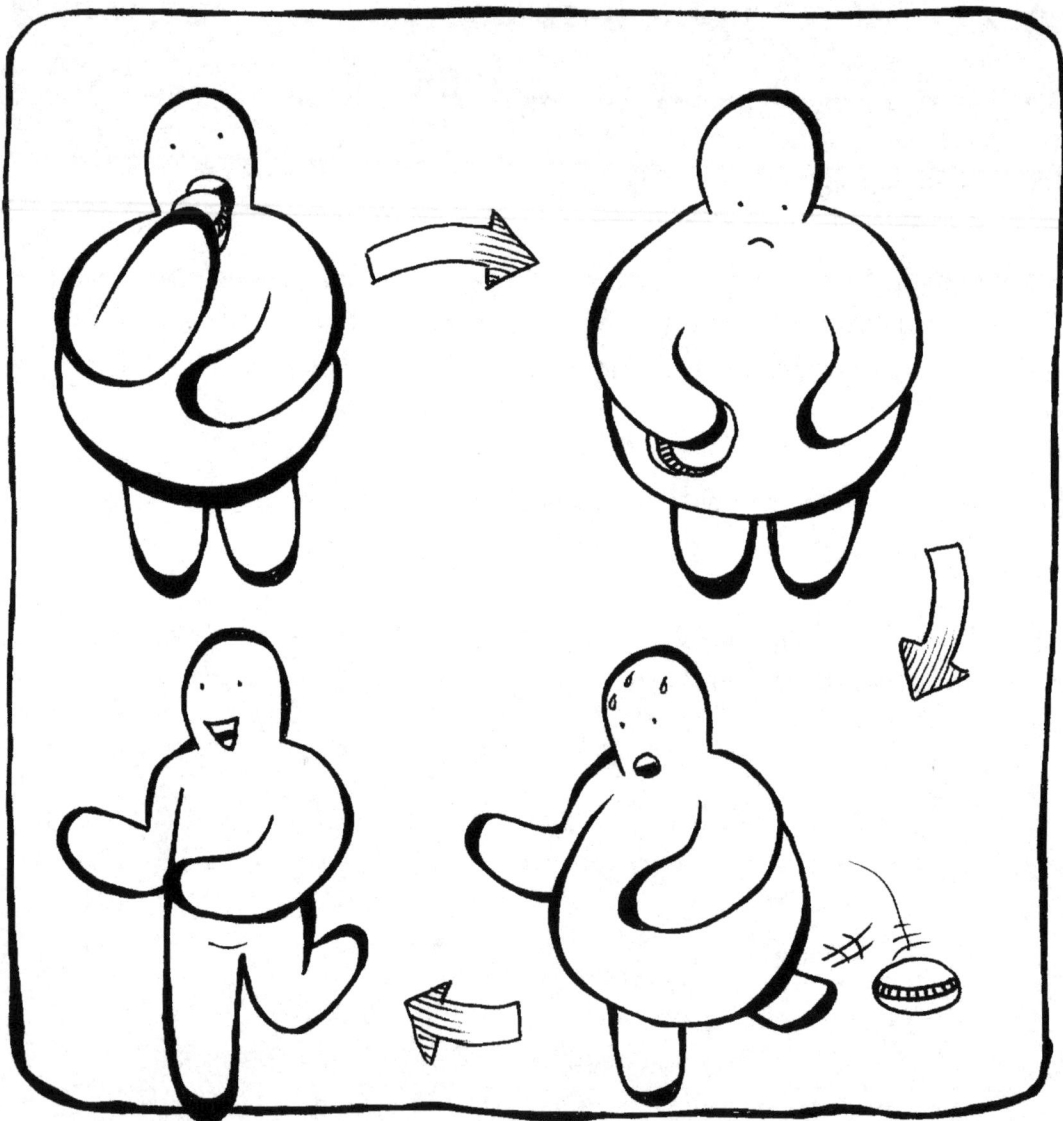

Day 22: draw a heart upon your lips

Our words reveal the thoughts of our hearts. Our words are the doorway to our soul. Have you ever listened to your own words?

During today, reflect upon the things which come out of your mouth - the things you might not consciously realise that you reveal about yourself. Are you pleased with what you hear?

The first stage of change is to become self aware. The second stage is to substitute something better for it. The final stage is to practise it so much that it becomes a natural part of who we are.

When Jesus spent forty days in the desert, He changed from His life as a carpenter, to the life of a Rabbi.

Change is always possible - even big change

Prayer: draw a heart on your lips and ask God to help your words to become agents of change today.

Reflections

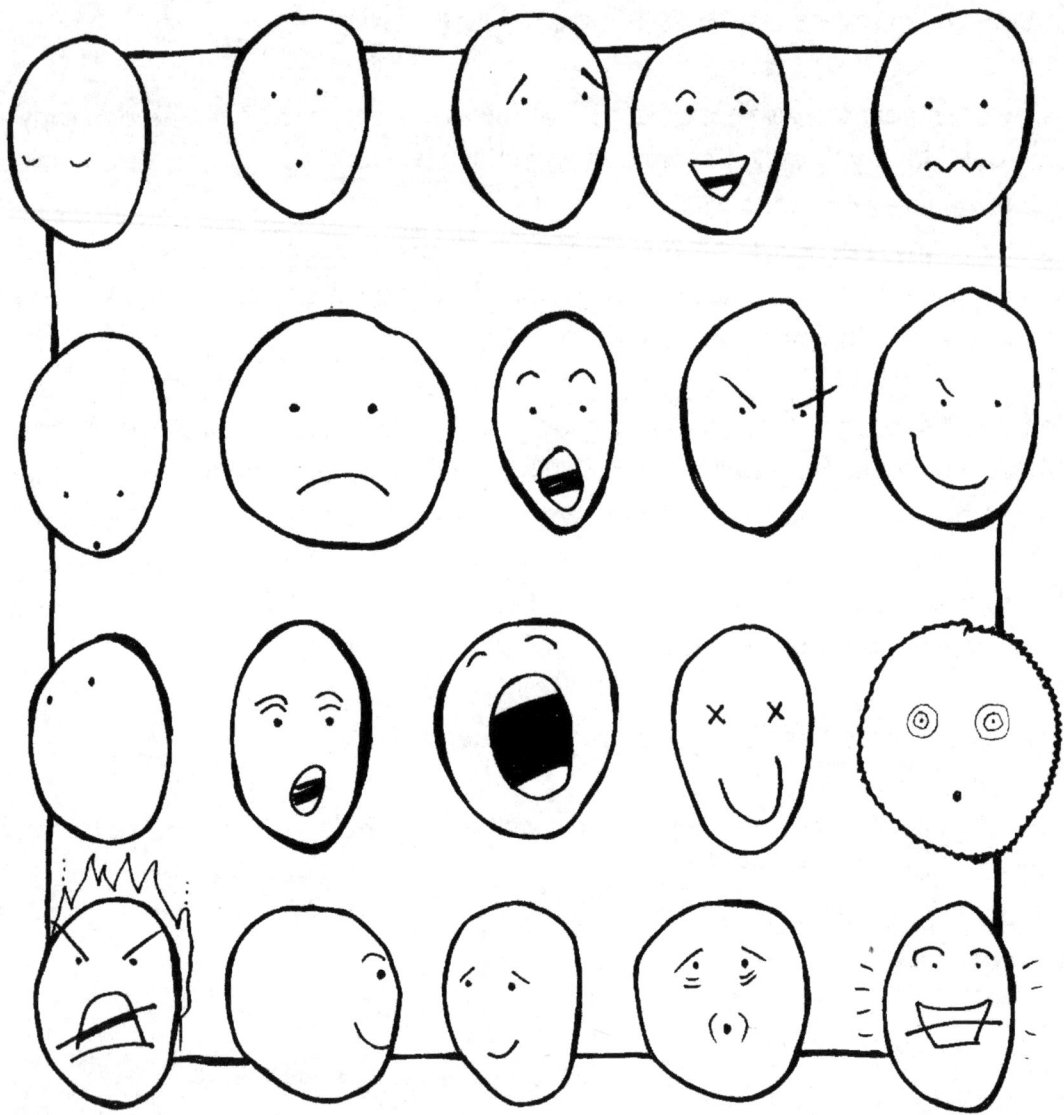

Day 23: write down all the feelings you remember experiencing yesterday

Being alone for any length of time makes us more aware of how we feel. In the course of a day we can feel content, lonely, desperate, rejected, angry, hyper, ill, popular, valued, passionate, sexy, successful, foolish, hated, loved and many more.

Which feelings can you recall yesterday not feeling?

When Jesus was in the desert there were no time pressures on Him, just His feelings as companions.

Which feelings do you think may have overwhelmed Him?

Action: as you go through today, be on the look out for those who are overwhelmed by their feelings.

Reflections

Day 24: find a noisy space for today's reflection

Go to a noisy place, the exact opposite of the desert Jesus went to. Try to concentrate on this text. Ask yourself why some people always like music on - noise in their 'day to day' lives.

Now find a quiet place and ask yourself which situation is easier for you to reflect in?

Which do you usually choose to be in when you have the freedom to choose? Do you flee silence or noise?

Make a conscious decision today to find value in both the noisy and quiet places.

Prayer: ask God to help you find Him in the noise and busyness too.

Reflections

Day 25: place a cold/ warm object against your cheek

A desert is too hot by day and too cold by night. It is a place of extremes. For some people we relate to, their lives are full of extremes.

Think of how you cope when you are rejected or loved by others - the two extreme reactions.

Did you reject others yesterday? Why?

Did you accept others yesterday? Why?

Action: today, choose to accept others as God chooses to accept you today, by valuing their company, regardless of their behaviour.

Reflections

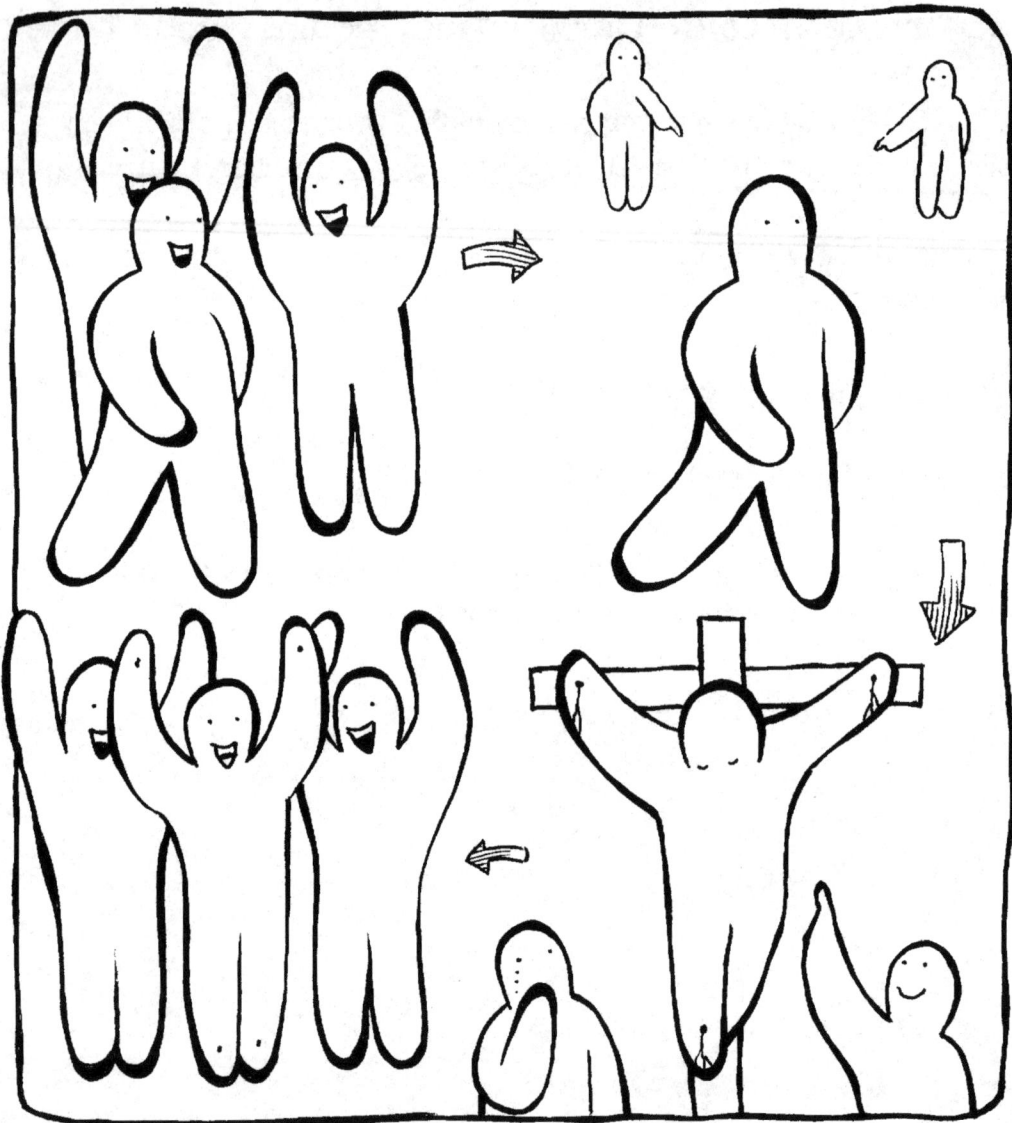

Day 26: reflect upon these words

'Easter - a place for popularity, death, abandonment and resurrection'.

Have you ever been through such extremes of feelings in a matter of days?

Consider your friends, family and colleagues. Someone from this group is probably in the midst of such turmoil. Do you know who it is?

Allow yourself time to think about who it might be.

How can you reach out to them? How can you help them?

If you were going through such up and down feelings, what would help you cope?

Jesus spent forty days alone knowing that one day He would be abandoned by even His disciples.

Prayer: Dear Lord, open my eyes to those who are struggling. Help me to support them.

Reflections

Day 27: touch each Blob in turn

The Blob by level 1 is someone you may say hello to today.

The Blob by level 2 is someone who may give you information today.

The Blob at level 3 may tell you their opinion today.

The Blob at level 4 may share their feelings with you.

The Blob at level 5 is your closest friend.

Pray for each one to grow closer to you today as you reveal yourself to them.

Reflections

Day 28: press your face against a towel or something soft

Feel how comforting it is.

Now touch something cold or rough, such as a mirror or sandpaper.

The desert is a harsh environment. We can become like it too, especially as others treat us with hostility.

Prayer: help us to be a warm, welcoming friend who loves and listens to all those around us. Lord, may we be like Jesus.

Action: during our day we may come into contact with harshness. Fight it with warm, open arms.

Reflections

Day 29: look at this picture

Imagine stepping out of your comfort zone today.

When Jesus went into the desert He was going into a place of isolation - not something most of us would choose. It required a degree of strength to make Himself vulnerable in that way.

Here is an exercise to try: during today, step into a vulnerable place. Find a quiet spot to look around at a group of people who might not know each other. Talk to one of them and try to strike up a conversation, make them feel accepted. They may reject you because they feel vulnerable too, but at least you will have tried.

The more you try the better you get at being able to include those who feel vulnerable, but it requires a degree of vulnerability on our part first.

Reflections

Day 30: write on this picture

Use pencil if you wish to do this again next year.

Write a list of your friends in tough situations upon the Blobs in this circle.

 Friends who need your prayers

Action/ prayer: touch each name and pray for them.

Ask God to step into their situations and guide them through it.

We are part of God's answer to prayer.

What ideas of how you can help them came to mind?

Reflections

Day 31: think of someone who is feeling very lonely

Think of someone who might appreciate a phone call.

The greatest way to value others is to give our time.

Action: call them and love them with your time and listening ear.

Reflections

Day 32: look at the journey each Blob went through

Each of us has been through a unique life, yet we often imagine that everyone has had similar experiences.

All of us carry wounds and scars. Some of these are physical, some emotional and some mental.

Some people are broken by these experiences: mental breakdowns, emotional breakdowns and physical breakdowns, which can include injuries.

Many thought Jesus was just the son of a carpenter. They didn't know Him fully.

Action: when you think of Jesus today, think of the parts you don't know - how He felt as a child growing up in Egypt, as a brother in a family, as a young man expected to become a carpenter, as a man with a mission surrounded by pretty girls who had fallen in love with Him, as a cross making carpenter, preparing the means of His own execution.

Prayer: ask God to help you to see the whole of those you meet, not just their present. Ask God to help you to see the whole of Him.

Reflections

Day 33: how many people did you touch yesterday?

There are some people who never touch another person in a whole day. Was that you yesterday?

In a desert, alone, there is no one to touch.

Have you ever spent a day alone without anyone to touch?

Do you think that you could?

Babies are touched and held so much of the time. It is the start of life.

The elderly are often untouched if they have lost their partner.

Where are you along the continuum?

Action: can you find a way to touch others in a loving way today who might not ever know a pat on the shoulder or a shake of the hand?

Prayer: reflect upon when God touched you yesterday.

Reflections

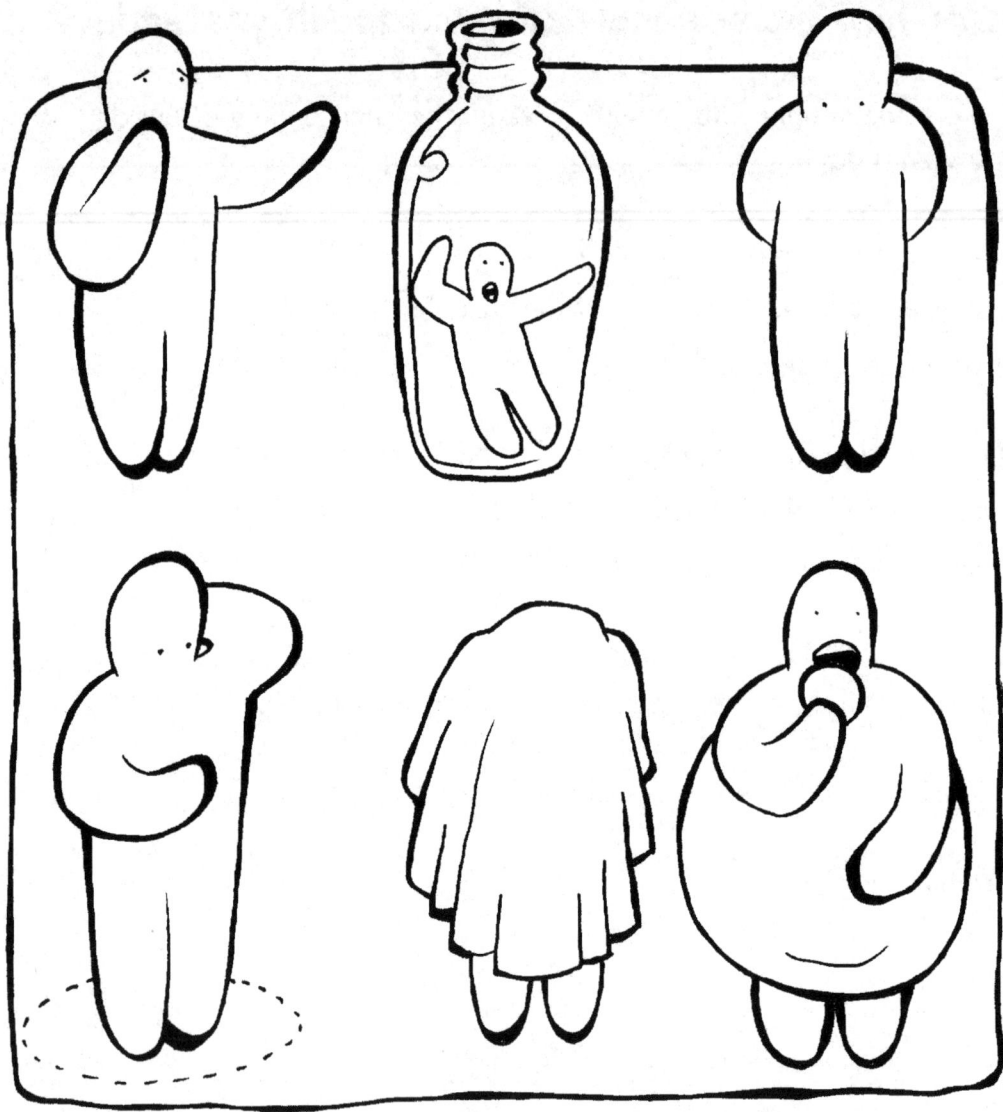

Day 34: look at these Blobs

Which ones do you feel need to be befriended most?

Can you give each one a name of a person that you know?

Action/ prayer: pray for opportunities to talk to them in the coming days and tick each one off as you manage it.

Reflections

Day 35: reflect upon these words

'The desert tests us to our limits and can even kill us'.

Jesus did not choose the desert, He was led there.

God led Him into a testing period of preparation as a mature adult, as a believer.

It tested Him to His limits.

Angels had to look after Him when it was all over.

He needed total care afterwards, such was His exhaustion.

Who are the angels in your life? Do you recognise them?

Jesus was able to allow angels to care for Him.

Who are you an angel to?

Is it someone who is truly unable to reciprocate?

Are you happy to care?

Reflections

Day 36: think of the last time that you were exhausted or run down

In the desert, Jesus was utterly exhausted. Even then, when He was close to death, the devil was unable to make Him sin.

Each of us have moments when we have irrational outbursts – they feel so unlike who we usually are.

Which is the area of life that triggers outbursts for you? Hunger? Anger? Loneliness? Tiredness? These are the usual trigger points.

Action: the next time you reach this point, watch what you do. Make a conscious decision to avoid the outbursts.

Prayer: bring these past outbursts into God's presence. Ask Him to change you from within so that you can avoid repeating these patterns.

Reflections

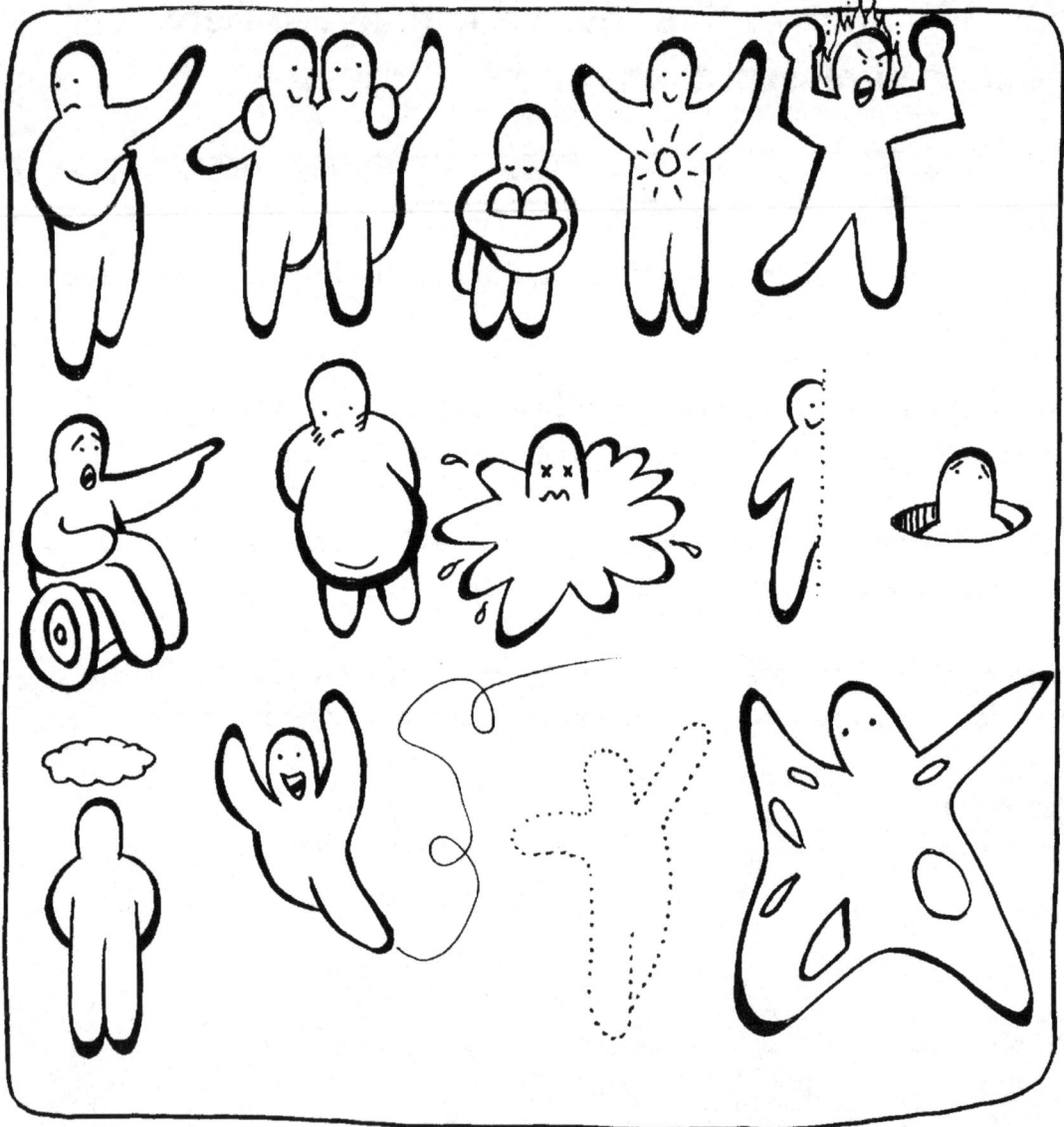

Day 37: colour in the Blobs

Colour in the Blob who you would like to love today. Touch that Blob and give them a name of someone you think that you might see in the course of the day.

Action: take time to ask questions of your friend, listen carefully to their answers without using your phone once during the conversation, and try to share yourself fully, including your feelings.

Prayer: ask God to make you a better 'people lover'

Reflections

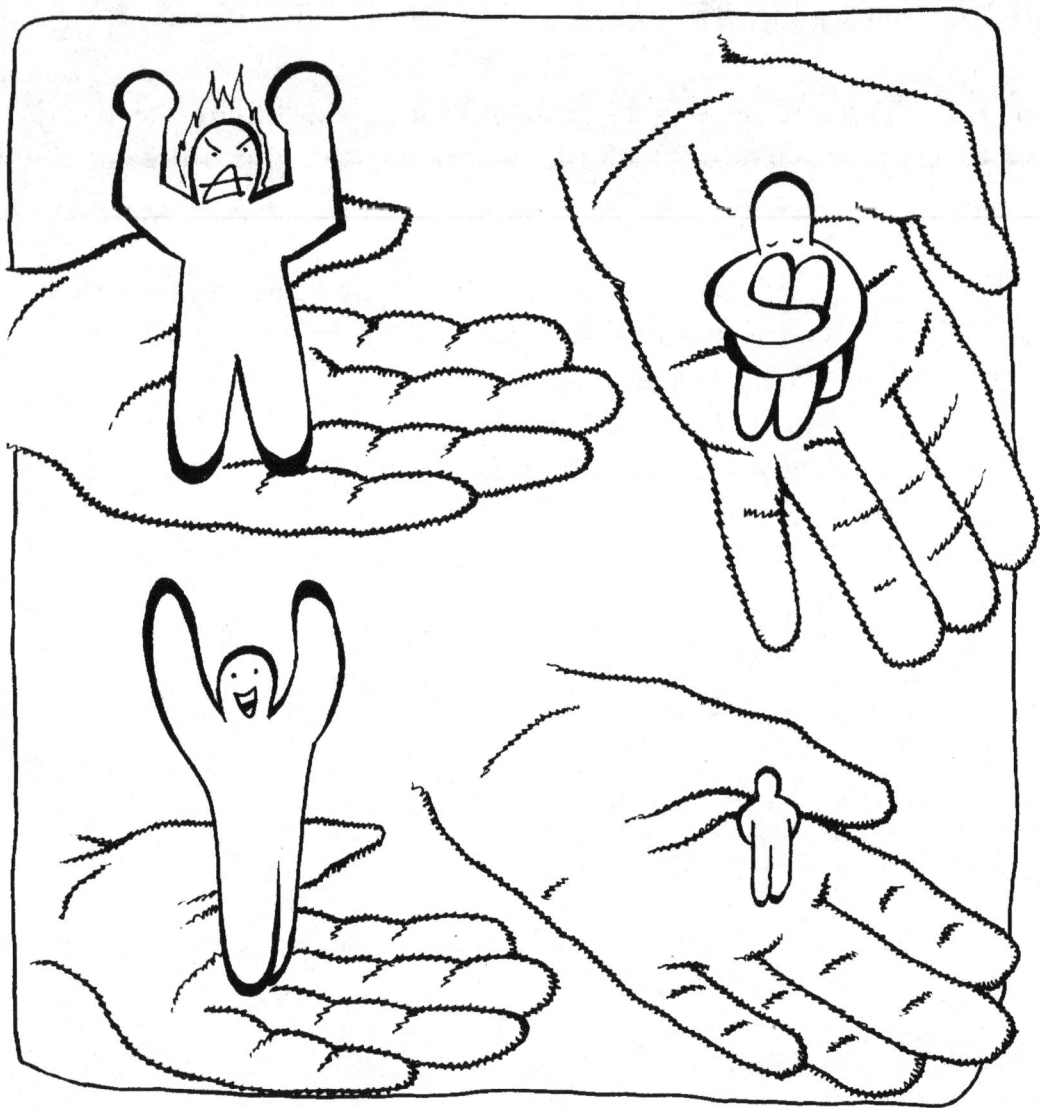

Day 38: touch each image of the Blobs in God's palm

When have you felt comforted by God?

When have you felt protected and loved? Was that recently?

Sometimes we don't recognise God's work in our life because we don't spend much time looking for it.

Prayer: thank God for the times He has helped you, and ask Him to make you more aware of those times.

Reflections

HO Me

Day 39: reflect upon these words

'L o v e = H o m e'

Where do we choose to call home?

Is it the place we really value?

In the desert, Jesus made His Father His home. His life reflected that decision. He spent forty days alone with His Father.

Can you bring love back into your family and friendships where it might have waned?

Prayer: ask God to be the centre of your life, and for His love to help you to make your family and friends feel special and valued.

Action: book in a time to go for a walk with someone in our family, to chat with them and discover what is upon their heart.

Reflections

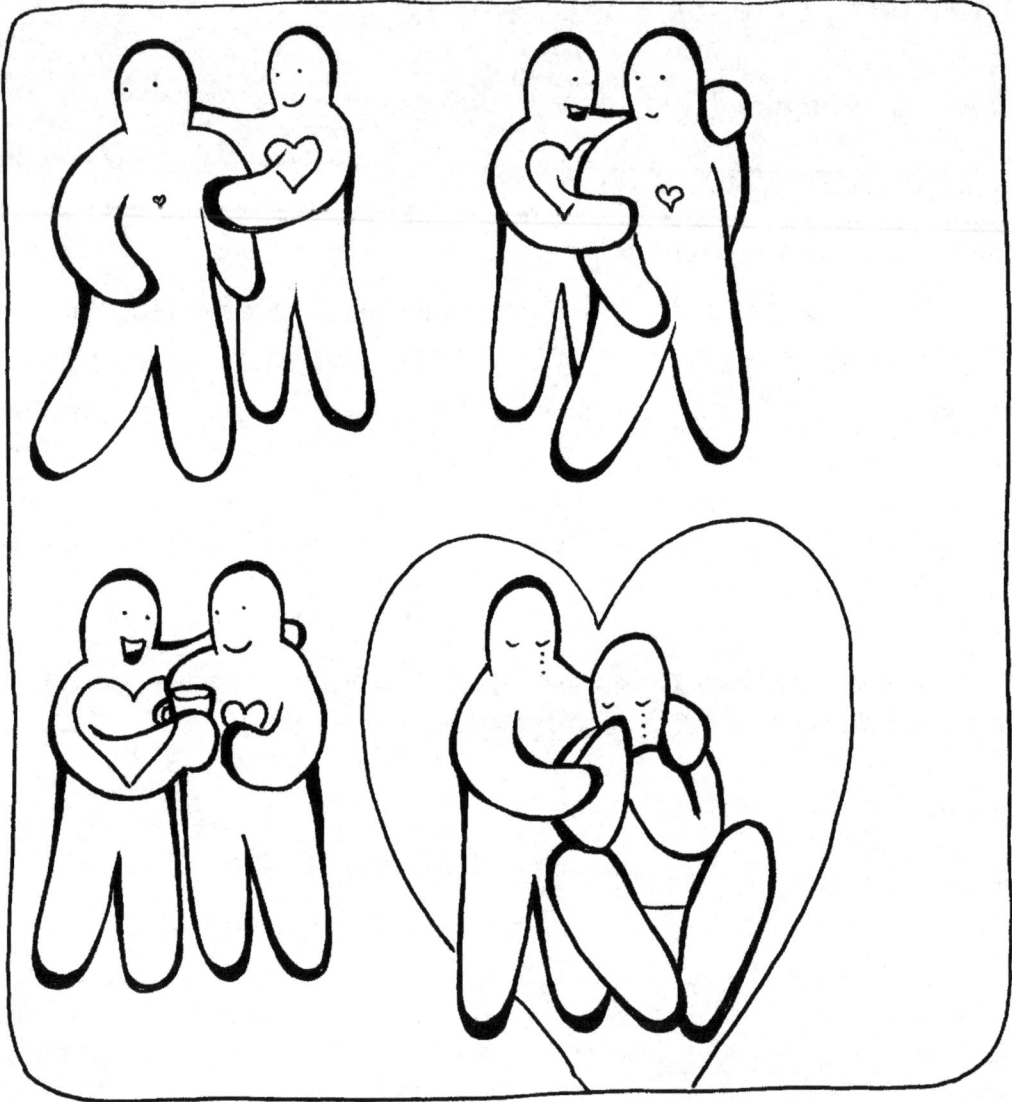

Day 40: breathe in deeply and exhale slowly five times with your eyes closed

Lent is coming to an end. For Jesus it was the start of his spiritual work. Each day is the start of our spiritual work.

For Francis of Assisi it involved kissing those whom he loved.

Are there those we can love with a kiss on the cheeks, with a word of kindness, with an affirming touch, or with a smile?

Action: try to find people to kiss, hug, speak to, touch and smile at today.

By doing so we become agents of change, instruments of grace.

Finally, although this book has come to an end, our life continues on. Each day we can be lovers - healing agents.

Take the principles in this book and use them to change ourselves and enrich the world we occupy.

Reflections

There are many other books in the blobtree.com range.

For example:

Blob Spirituality

The Blob Bible

You are a beautiful human person

Between the Bars

Gutter Feelings

Please visit the website www.lulu.com and search for The Blob Tree for more books about change.

You can also find a wide range of books for sale at www.speechmark.co.uk

For example:

The Big Book of Blob Trees

The Blob Manual

Blob Feelings

Blob Angrr

Ian and Pip